The 76th Emmy

Awards:

A detailed review of

the event

Anthony Walter

Table of Content

Introduction

Overview of the 76th Emmy Awards

The 76th Emmy Awards, held on September 9, 2024, at L.A.'s Peacock Theater, was a grand celebration of television excellence. This annual event, presented by the Academy of Television Arts & Sciences, honors outstanding achievements in the television industry, spotlighting the best in drama, comedy, limited series, variety, and reality programming.

This year's ceremony stood out for its remarkable array of winners and record-breaking achievements. The evening was marked by a mix of expected victories and surprising upsets, reflecting the evolving landscape of television.

Disney led the night with a historic total of 60 Emmy wins, underlining its dominance in the entertainment industry. Notably, the awards showcased the versatility and depth of contemporary television, highlighting both established favorites and innovative newcomers.

The Ceremony and Hosts:

Hosted by Eugene and Dan Levy, the ceremony was a blend of humor, elegance, and celebration. Eugene Levy, known for his sharp wit and distinctive comedic style, along with his son Dan Levy, brought a fresh and engaging energy to the event. Their hosting was characterized by a mix of light-hearted jokes, insightful commentary, and heartfelt tributes to the winners and nominees.

The Peacock Theater, known for its modern architecture and state-of-the-art facilities, provided a fitting backdrop for the event. The venue's grandeur was complemented by elaborate stage designs and dazzling performances, making it a night to remember for both attendees and viewers at home.

Key Moments and Highlights:

One of the most talked-about highlights of the evening was the triumph of "The Bear," which set a new record for the most Emmy wins in a single season for a comedy series. The show's impressive haul included awards for best lead actor, best supporting actress, best supporting actor, and best directing, further cementing its status as a critical and audience favorite.

Another major highlight was "Shogun"'s historic sweep in the drama categories. The series not only won best drama series but also saw its lead actors, Anna Sawai and Hiroyuki Sanada, become the first Japanese actors to win Emmys in their respective categories. This achievement was a significant milestone in the industry, reflecting the growing diversity and global reach of television storytelling.

In the limited series category, "Baby Reindeer" emerged as a standout, securing multiple awards including best limited or anthology series and acting honors for Richard Gadd and Jessica Gunning. This series' success underscored the strong storytelling and compelling performances that continue to define the genre.

Overall Impact:

The 76th Emmys highlighted the changing dynamics of television. The emphasis on diverse voices and international content was evident in the winners and nominees, showcasing a broader spectrum of stories and talents. The event also underscored the growing importance of streaming platforms, with many winners and nominees coming from digital-first productions.

Significance and Impact of the Awards

The significance of the 76th Emmy Awards extends beyond just the accolades given to individuals and productions. It represents a pivotal moment in the evolution of television, reflecting broader trends and shifts within the industry.

A Celebration of Diversity and Inclusion:
One of the most notable aspects of the 76th Emmys was the emphasis on diversity and inclusion. The recognition of "Shogun"'s Japanese actors, Anna Sawai and Hiroyuki Sanada, as well as Liza Colón-Zayas becoming

the first Latina to win best supporting actress in a comedy series, marked a significant step forward in celebrating underrepresented voices in television. These achievements highlight the growing appreciation for diverse perspectives and the importance of inclusivity in storytelling.

The success of shows like "The Bear" and "Baby Reindeer" also reflects the industry's expanding definition of quality content. These series, which feature unique narratives and diverse casts, resonated strongly with audiences and critics alike, demonstrating that innovation and authenticity are highly valued.

The Rise of Streaming Platforms:

The 76th Emmys further underscored the dominance of streaming platforms in the television landscape. With Disney, Netflix, and Apple TV+ leading the pack in terms of wins and nominations, it is clear that digital platforms are now central players in the industry. The success of streaming content at the Emmys highlights the shift from traditional broadcast and cable networks to digital-first strategies, influencing how content is produced, distributed, and consumed.

Setting New Standards:

The awards ceremony also set new standards for excellence and innovation in television. The record-breaking achievements of shows like "The Bear" and the diverse wins across various categories illustrate a shift towards recognizing and rewarding excellence in all its forms. These new benchmarks reflect an evolving industry that values creativity, originality, and inclusivity.

Industry Trends and Future Directions:

The impact of the 76th Emmys will likely be felt for years to come, as it signals the direction in which the television industry is heading. The increased focus on international content, diverse storytelling, and streaming platforms will continue to shape future productions and awards considerations.

Moreover, the recognition of unconventional shows and performances suggests a growing willingness to embrace new formats and narratives. This trend is indicative of a broader cultural shift towards valuing originality and inclusivity in media.

Conclusion

The 76th Emmy Awards were more than just a celebration of television; they were a reflection of the industry's ongoing transformation. By honoring a wide range of voices and stories, the Emmys showcased the richness and diversity of contemporary television. The awards not only celebrated past achievements but also set the stage for future innovation and inclusivity, shaping the future of the industry in meaningful ways.

Chapter One: The Ceremony

Date and Venue

The 76th Annual Emmy Awards, a pinnacle event in the television industry, was held on September 15, 2024, at the glamorous Peacock Theatre in Los Angeles. The choice of venue and timing underscored the event's significance and tradition. The Peacock Theatre, known for its modern design and luxurious amenities, provided an ideal setting for this prestigious occasion, reflecting the high standards of the Emmy Awards.

The ceremony took place in mid-September, a strategic choice that aligns with the Emmys' long-standing tradition of celebrating the best in television from the previous year. This timing allows the awards to serve as a prelude to the upcoming fall television season, generating buzz and excitement in the industry. The mid-September date also provides a moment of reflection on the television year that was, offering a chance to honor the creative achievements and milestones that have defined the landscape of TV.

The Peacock Theatre, located in the heart of Los Angeles, added an extra layer of sophistication to the event. Its state-of-the-art facilities and striking architecture made it a fitting venue for the Emmys, emphasizing the importance of the occasion and providing a backdrop that enhanced the overall glamour of the evening. The theatre's spacious interior and modern design allowed for an elegant and comfortable environment, accommodating the high-profile attendees and ensuring a seamless experience for all involved.

Hosts and Key Moments

The 76th Emmy Awards were hosted by Eugene Levy and Dan Levy, a dynamic duo whose selection brought both excitement and a sense of familiarity to the event. Eugene Levy, known for his work on "Schitt's Creek," and his son Dan Levy, who also gained acclaim for the same show, were celebrated for their wit, charm, and deep connection to the television industry. Their hosting style was a blend of humor and heartfelt commentary, setting a lively and engaging tone for the evening.

One of the most memorable moments of the ceremony was the surprise victory of "Hacks" for Best Comedy Series, beating out the previous year's winner, "The Bear." This unexpected outcome highlighted the unpredictability of the Emmys and showcased the shifting dynamics within the television landscape. The win for "Hacks" was particularly notable for its impact on the comedy genre and its recognition of fresh, innovative storytelling.

Another key moment was the historic win of Liza Colón-Zayas for Best Supporting Actress in a Comedy Series. Her victory was significant as she became the first Latina to win in this category, marking a milestone in the Emmys' history and reflecting the ongoing push for greater diversity and representation in the industry. Her emotional acceptance speech resonated with many, celebrating not just her own achievement but also the broader progress toward inclusivity in television.

The ceremony also featured a series of poignant and celebratory speeches from winners across various categories. These speeches offered insights into the creative processes behind the nominated works and provided a platform for expressing gratitude to the teams and supporters who contributed to their success. The acceptance speeches were a highlight of the evening, adding a personal touch to the formal awards presentations and emphasizing the collaborative nature of television production.

Musical performances and comedic sketches were interspersed throughout the ceremony, enhancing the overall entertainment value. These segments provided light-hearted moments and showcased the talents of performers beyond their usual roles, adding a layer of fun and variety to the evening. The carefully curated entertainment segments contributed to the overall success of the event, making it an engaging experience for both the live audience and viewers at home.

<u>Major Themes and Highlights</u>

The 76th Emmy Awards underscored several major themes that have been increasingly prominent in the television industry. One of the most significant themes was diversity and representation. The historic win by Liza Colón-Zayas highlighted the Emmys' focus on recognizing and celebrating talent from diverse backgrounds. This emphasis on inclusivity reflects a broader industry trend toward acknowledging and valuing the contributions of underrepresented groups in television.

Another major theme was the continued rise of streaming platforms as dominant forces in the television landscape. Disney's record-breaking

60 wins, including numerous accolades for its streaming content, illustrated the shifting dynamics of television consumption. The success of streaming services like Hulu and Netflix highlights the growing influence of digital platforms and their ability to produce high-quality, innovative content that resonates with audiences.

The ceremony also celebrated the evolving nature of storytelling and production quality in television. Shows like "Shogun" and "Baby Reindeer" received multiple awards, reflecting the industry's increasing appreciation for unique narratives and high production values. These highlights emphasize the Emmys' role in recognizing and rewarding creative excellence across various genres and formats.

Overall, the 76th Emmy Awards showcased a blend of tradition and innovation, celebrating the best of television while also reflecting the changes and advancements within the industry. The event successfully honored the achievements of the past year while setting the stage for the future of television, making it a memorable and impactful occasion for all involved.

Chapter Two:
Record-Breaking Wins

Disney's Record-Breaking Achievements

The 76th Emmy Awards marked a historic moment for Disney, as the entertainment giant set a new benchmark with a staggering 60 wins across various categories. This unprecedented achievement not only underscored Disney's dominance in the television industry but also highlighted the company's successful expansion into streaming and digital content.

Disney's record-breaking performance was a testament to its diverse portfolio, which spans traditional TV networks, cable channels, and its rapidly growing streaming platforms. The company's success was fueled by its high-quality programming and innovative content strategies, which have captured the imagination of audiences worldwide.

A significant portion of Disney's wins came from its streaming services, particularly Disney+ and Hulu. These platforms have become crucial players in the TV landscape, producing content that resonates with a wide range of viewers. Disney's strategy of investing heavily in original programming and acquiring high-profile content has paid off, as evidenced by the numerous awards garnered across different genres and categories.

The achievements of Disney at the Emmys also reflect the company's ability to adapt and thrive in a competitive media environment. By leveraging its vast resources and creative talent, Disney has maintained its position as a leading force in entertainment. The record number of wins is not just a reflection of the company's current success but also a signal of its ongoing commitment to excellence and innovation in television production.

The Bear's Historic Wins

"The Bear," an acclaimed FX series, achieved a remarkable milestone at the 76th Emmy Awards by setting a new record for the most wins in a single season for a comedy series. The show secured an impressive 11 awards, surpassing its previous record of 10 wins from the previous year. This extraordinary achievement highlights the show's continued impact and its significant contribution to the comedy genre.

The Bear's success was fueled by its compelling storytelling, memorable characters, and high-caliber performances. The series' ability to blend humor with poignant moments resonated with both critics and audiences, cementing its place as a standout in a crowded field of television comedies.

Jeremy Allen White's win for Best Lead Actor in a Comedy Series was one of the show's crowning achievements. White's portrayal of a young chef navigating the challenges of a restaurant kitchen was widely praised for its depth and authenticity. His win reflected the show's strong performances and its ability to capture the nuances of its characters.

Additionally, the recognition of Liza Colón-Zayas as Best Supporting Actress in a Comedy Series was historic, marking her as the first Latina to win in this category. Her win was a significant milestone for the Emmys, reflecting the ongoing efforts to promote diversity and representation within the industry.

The Bear's record-setting performance at the Emmys not only celebrated its creative and artistic accomplishments but also highlighted its influence on the comedy landscape. The series' ability to consistently deliver quality content and connect with audiences has solidified its legacy as a groundbreaking show in television history.

Shogun's Groundbreaking Awards

"Shogun," the FX drama series based on James Clavell's epic novel, achieved groundbreaking success at the 76th Emmy Awards with four major wins, including Best Drama Series. The show's victory in this highly competitive category was a testament to its exceptional production values and its ability to bring a historical narrative to life with great authenticity and depth.

One of the most notable aspects of Shogun's success was the historic win by Anna Sawai for Best Actress in a Drama Series. Sawai's portrayal of a complex and resilient character marked her as the first Japanese actress to win in this category. Her performance was widely acclaimed for its emotional depth and versatility, contributing significantly to the show's overall success.

Hiroyuki Sanada's win for Best Actor in a Drama Series was another significant achievement for Shogun. Sanada's portrayal of a powerful and nuanced character showcased his exceptional acting skills and further solidified the show's reputation for high-quality performances.

Shogun's success at the Emmys was also marked by Frederick E.O. Toye's win for Best Directing for a Drama Series. Toye's direction played a crucial role in bringing the epic tale to life, capturing the intricate details and historical context of the narrative while maintaining a compelling and engaging storyline.

The show's ability to achieve critical acclaim and industry recognition for its storytelling, performances, and direction underscored its groundbreaking impact on television. Shogun's success at the Emmys highlighted the importance of historical and culturally significant narratives in modern television and set a new standard for excellence in the drama genre.

Baby Reindeer's Success

"Baby Reindeer," the limited series that captivated audiences with its unique storytelling and powerful performances, achieved remarkable success at the 76th Emmy Awards. The series garnered four wins, including Best Limited or Anthology Series, making it one of the standout successes of the evening.

Richard Gadd, the lead actor in Baby Reindeer, was honored with the award for Best Actor in a Limited or Anthology Series or Movie. Gadd's performance was widely praised for its depth and emotional range, contributing significantly to the series' critical acclaim. His win was a testament to his skillful portrayal of a complex character and his ability to connect with audiences on a profound level.

In addition to Gadd's win, Baby Reindeer also received the award for Best Writing in the Limited or Anthology Series or Movie category. Richard Gadd's role as a writer further showcased his versatility and talent, contributing to the series' overall success and its ability to deliver compelling and thought-provoking content.

Jessica Gunning's win for Best Supporting Actress in a Limited or Anthology Series or Movie was another highlight of Baby Reindeer's success. Gunning's performance added depth and nuance to the series, complementing the lead performances and enhancing the overall storytelling.

The success of Baby Reindeer at the Emmys underscored the series' impact on the limited series genre and its ability to deliver high-quality, engaging content. The awards recognized not only the individual performances but also the collective efforts of the cast and crew in creating a memorable and impactful series.

Overall, the record-breaking achievements of Disney, the historic wins of The Bear, the groundbreaking success of Shogun, and the triumph of Baby Reindeer at the 76th Emmy Awards highlighted the diverse and dynamic nature of television storytelling. Each of these successes contributed to the celebration of excellence in the industry and showcased the continuing evolution and innovation within the world of television.

Chapter Three: Drama Series

Best Drama Series: Shogun

The 76th Emmy Awards showcased "Shogun" as the standout winner in the Best Drama Series category, cementing its place as a monumental achievement in television history. Adapted from James Clavell's iconic novel, "Shogun" transported viewers to the 17th century, weaving a tale of cultural clash and personal struggle through the lens of historical fiction. The show's victory in this category was a reflection of its exceptional storytelling, meticulous attention to historical detail, and compelling character development.

"Shogun" stood out in a highly competitive field of drama series for several reasons. Its narrative, set against the backdrop of Japan's feudal era, was both ambitious and intricate. The series managed to capture the essence of Clavell's novel while presenting it in a way that felt both accessible and relevant to contemporary audiences. The show's ability to blend historical accuracy with dramatic storytelling allowed it to resonate deeply with viewers and critics alike.

The production values of "Shogun" also contributed significantly to its success. The series' attention to detail in costume design, set decoration, and cinematography created a visually stunning experience that transported viewers to a different time and place. This high level of craftsmanship, combined with a strong script and a talented cast, made "Shogun" a standout entry in the drama category.

Best Actor in a Drama Series: Hiroyuki Sanada

Hiroyuki Sanada's win for Best Actor in a Drama Series was a pivotal moment at the 76th Emmys. Sanada's portrayal of the powerful and enigmatic Lord Toranaga in "Shogun" was widely acclaimed for its depth and complexity. His performance brought to life a character who is both a formidable leader and a deeply flawed human being, navigating the treacherous waters of political intrigue and personal ambition.

Sanada's portrayal was marked by its subtlety and nuance. He effectively captured the inner conflicts of his character, balancing strength and vulnerability in a way that drew viewers into the world of "Shogun." His ability to convey a wide range of emotions, from intense resolve to introspective doubt, added layers of depth to the series and elevated its dramatic impact.

The recognition of Sanada's performance at the Emmys was a testament to his skill and dedication as an actor. His win not only celebrated his individual achievement but also highlighted the exceptional quality of the acting talent involved in "Shogun." Sanada's portrayal was integral to the series' success and its ability to engage and captivate audiences.

Best Actress in a Drama Series: Anna Sawai

Anna Sawai's victory for Best Actress in a Drama Series was another significant highlight at the 76th Emmy Awards. Sawai's role as Lady Mariko in "Shogun" showcased her remarkable talent and marked her as the first Japanese actress to win in this category. Her performance was celebrated for its emotional depth, strength, and authenticity, making her a standout in a competitive field.

Sawai's portrayal of Lady Mariko was a powerful representation of a woman navigating the complexities of a patriarchal society while grappling with her own personal dilemmas. Her performance captured the character's resilience, intelligence, and emotional turmoil, adding significant depth to the series' narrative. Sawai's ability to convey both the strength and vulnerability of her character resonated deeply with audiences and critics alike.

The recognition of Sawai's performance was not only a personal achievement but also a milestone for diversity and representation in the industry. Her win underscored the importance of recognizing and celebrating the contributions of actors from diverse backgrounds, and it highlighted the growing inclusivity within the television industry.

Best Supporting Actor in a Drama Series: Billy Crudup

Billy Crudup's win for Best Supporting Actor in a Drama Series was another notable achievement at the 76th Emmys. Crudup's performance in "The Morning Show" was widely praised for its depth and complexity. His portrayal of Cory Ellison, a shrewd and ambitious network executive, added a compelling layer to the series' exploration of media ethics and personal ambition.

Crudup's performance was characterized by its intensity and precision. He effectively captured the character's manipulative tendencies and underlying vulnerability, creating a multidimensional portrayal that stood out among his peers. His ability to bring nuance and authenticity to his role was a key factor in his success at the Emmys.

The recognition of Crudup's performance highlighted the strength of the supporting cast in "The Morning Show" and underscored the importance of strong character development in ensemble-driven dramas. His win was a testament to his skill and the overall quality of the series.

Best Supporting Actress in a Drama Series: Elizabeth Debicki

Elizabeth Debicki's win for Best Supporting Actress in a Drama Series was a major highlight of the 76th Emmys. Her performance in "The

Crown" was celebrated for its grace and complexity, showcasing her ability to bring depth and nuance to her role as Princess Diana. Debicki's portrayal was a key factor in the series' continued success and critical acclaim.

Debicki's performance was marked by its emotional resonance and authenticity. She effectively captured the essence of Princess Diana, portraying her with both dignity and vulnerability. Her ability to convey the character's personal struggles and public persona added significant depth to "The Crown" and contributed to the series' overall impact.

The recognition of Debicki's performance was a testament to her exceptional talent and the high quality of the acting in "The Crown." Her win highlighted the importance of strong supporting performances in enhancing the overall narrative of a drama series.

Best Directing for a Drama Series: Frederick E.O. Toye

Frederick E.O. Toye's win for Best Directing for a Drama Series was a significant achievement at the 76th Emmys. Toye's work on "Shogun" was widely praised for its craftsmanship and attention to detail. His direction played a crucial role in bringing the series' intricate narrative and historical context to life.

Toye's direction was characterized by its meticulous attention to detail and its ability to create a visually stunning and emotionally engaging experience. He effectively captured the complexities of the story and the nuances of the characters, enhancing the overall impact of the series. His ability to balance historical accuracy with dramatic storytelling was a key factor in the series' success.

The recognition of Toye's direction underscored the importance of strong visual and narrative direction in creating compelling drama. His win celebrated his skill and the overall quality of the production, highlighting the role of direction in shaping the success of a drama series.

Analysis of Winning Shows and Performances

The 76th Emmy Awards highlighted several standout performances and series in the drama category. "Shogun" emerged as a major winner, with its success reflecting its exceptional storytelling, high production values, and strong performances. The series' ability to capture a historical narrative with both accuracy and dramatic impact set it apart in a competitive field.

The individual wins for Hiroyuki Sanada and Anna Sawai underscored the high caliber of acting in "Shogun." Sanada's portrayal of Lord Toranaga and Sawai's role as Lady Mariko were integral to the series' success, showcasing their exceptional talent and depth. Their performances brought a new level of complexity and emotional resonance to the series, contributing significantly to its critical acclaim.

In contrast, the wins for Billy Crudup and Elizabeth Debicki highlighted the strength of supporting performances in drama series. Crudup's portrayal in "The Morning Show" and Debicki's role in "The Crown" added depth and nuance to their respective series, demonstrating the importance of strong supporting roles in enhancing the overall narrative.

Frederick E.O. Toye's win for Best Directing in a Drama Series emphasized the crucial role of direction in shaping the success of a drama series. His work on "Shogun" was instrumental in bringing the series' intricate narrative and historical context to life, highlighting the importance of skilled direction in creating compelling television.

Overall, the 76th Emmy Awards celebrated a diverse range of achievements in the drama category, recognizing the exceptional talent and creativity that contribute to the success of television drama. The wins for "Shogun" and its cast, along with the recognition of other standout performances, underscored the continued evolution and innovation within the genre.

Chapter Four: Comedy Series

Best Comedy Series: Hacks

The 76th Emmy Awards saw "Hacks" take home the prestigious title of Best Comedy Series, affirming its status as a standout in the realm of television comedy. Created by Lucia Aniello, Paul W. Downs, and Jen Statsky, "Hacks" offers a fresh and incisive look at the world of stand-up comedy through its dynamic lead characters and sharp writing.

The series centers around the tumultuous relationship between Deborah Vance, a legendary stand-up comic struggling to remain relevant, and Ava Daniels, a young and edgy writer. What sets "Hacks" apart is its ability to blend humor with poignant moments, exploring themes of generational conflict, professional struggles, and personal growth. The show masterfully balances comedic elements with emotional depth, resulting in a series that resonates with both laughter and introspection.

"Hacks" impressed critics and audiences alike with its sharp dialogue, clever satire, and well-rounded characters. The series delves into the complexities of the comedy world, showcasing the challenges faced by performers as they navigate evolving tastes and industry pressures. Its win for Best Comedy Series was a recognition of its innovative approach to comedy, strong character development, and the seamless integration of humor with meaningful storytelling.

Best Actor in a Comedy Series: Jeremy Allen White

Jeremy Allen White's victory for Best Actor in a Comedy Series was a notable highlight of the 76th Emmys. White's performance in "The Bear" captivated audiences with its blend of intensity and humor. In the series, White portrays Carmy Berzatto, a talented but troubled chef trying to turn around a failing restaurant while managing personal demons.

White's portrayal of Carmy was marked by its raw authenticity and emotional depth. He navigated the character's highs and lows with a nuanced approach, capturing the intricacies of Carmy's struggle with both his professional and personal life. His ability to convey a range of emotions—from frustration and despair to moments of triumph—was a testament to his acting prowess.

The recognition of White's performance at the Emmys celebrated his skill in bringing a complex character to life. His win also underscored the strength of "The Bear" as a series that combines comedy with serious themes, and highlighted White's ability to anchor the show with his compelling performance.

Best Actress in a Comedy Series: Jean Smart

Jean Smart's win for Best Actress in a Comedy Series was a well-deserved accolade for her role in "Hacks." Smart's portrayal of Deborah Vance was widely praised for its depth, humor, and emotional resonance. As a seasoned comedian grappling with the challenges of staying relevant, Smart brought both vulnerability and strength to her character.

Smart's performance was characterized by its wit and nuance. She effectively captured the complexity of Deborah Vance, a woman whose sharp comedic exterior masks her personal insecurities and struggles. Her portrayal brought a compelling mix of humor and heart to the role, making Deborah Vance one of the most memorable characters on television.

The recognition of Smart's performance at the Emmys not only celebrated her exceptional talent but also highlighted the strength of "Hacks" as a series that showcases the power of great acting in enhancing comedic storytelling. Smart's win underscored her status as one of the leading actresses in comedy and celebrated her contribution to the success of "Hacks."

Best Supporting Actor in a Comedy Series: Ebon Moss-Bachrach

Ebon Moss-Bachrach's win for Best Supporting Actor in a Comedy Series was a notable achievement for his role in "The Bear." Moss-Bachrach's portrayal of Richie Jerimovich, a character with a complex blend of humor and pathos, added significant depth to the series. His performance as the troubled, yet endearing, sous-chef provided a crucial counterbalance to Jeremy Allen White's character.

Moss-Bachrach's ability to infuse his role with both comedic timing and emotional weight was a key factor in his success at the Emmys. His portrayal of Richie captured the character's struggles and growth, contributing to the overall dynamic of "The Bear." His performance was instrumental in adding layers to the series' narrative and enhancing its appeal to audiences.

The recognition of Moss-Bachrach's performance highlighted the importance of strong supporting roles in comedy series and underscored the quality of the ensemble cast in "The Bear." His win celebrated his contribution to the show and his ability to elevate the series through his nuanced performance.

Best Supporting Actress in a Comedy Series: Liza Colón-Zayas

Liza Colón-Zayas's win for Best Supporting Actress in a Comedy Series was a significant highlight of the 76th Emmys. Colón-Zayas's performance in "Hacks" as the charismatic and supportive character added a layer of authenticity and warmth to the series. Her role as the loyal friend and fellow comedian played a key part in the series' exploration of personal and professional dynamics in the comedy world.

Colón-Zayas's performance was marked by its naturalism and depth. She brought a genuine sense of warmth and relatability to her role, enhancing the series' portrayal of the comedy community. Her ability to convey both humor and heartfelt moments made her a standout in the supporting category.

The recognition of Colón-Zayas's performance celebrated her talent and the strength of the supporting cast in "Hacks." Her win underscored the importance of strong supporting roles in enhancing the overall quality of a comedy series and highlighted her contribution to the show's success.

Best Directing for a Comedy Series: Christopher Storer

Christopher Storer's win for Best Directing for a Comedy Series was a well-deserved accolade for his work on "The Bear." Storer's direction was integral to the series' ability to blend comedy with dramatic elements, creating a nuanced and compelling viewing experience. His skillful direction played a crucial role in shaping the series' tone and narrative.

Storer's approach to directing "The Bear" was characterized by its attention to detail and its ability to balance humor with more serious themes. His direction effectively captured the intensity of the kitchen environment while also highlighting the personal struggles of the characters. This blend of dramatic and comedic elements was a key factor in the series' success and critical acclaim.

The recognition of Storer's direction at the Emmys celebrated his contribution to the show and highlighted the role of skilled direction in creating a successful comedy series. His win underscored the importance of effective storytelling and direction in enhancing the overall impact of a television series.

Analysis of Winning Shows and Performances

The 76th Emmy Awards celebrated a diverse range of achievements in the comedy category, with "Hacks" and "The Bear" emerging as standout winners. "Hacks" was recognized for its innovative approach to comedy and its strong performances, particularly by Jean Smart and

Liza Colón-Zayas. The series' ability to blend humor with emotional depth made it a deserving winner in the Best Comedy Series category.

Jeremy Allen White's win for "The Bear" highlighted his exceptional performance as a troubled chef, capturing both the comedic and dramatic elements of the role. The series' success, combined with Ebon Moss-Bachrach's recognition for his supporting role and Christopher Storer's directing win, underscored the strength of the show's overall production.

The recognition of individual performances and directing in the comedy category reflected the continued evolution of the genre. The wins for actors and directors showcased the importance of nuanced performances and skilled direction in creating impactful comedy. Overall, the 76th Emmys celebrated a range of comedic achievements, highlighting the ongoing innovation and talent within the industry.

Chapter Five: Limited or Anthology Series

Best Limited or Anthology Series: Baby Reindeer

The 76th Emmy Awards honored "Baby Reindeer" with the prestigious title of Best Limited or Anthology Series, acknowledging its unique storytelling and exceptional execution. This series, crafted by a talented creative team, explored a gripping and emotionally charged narrative that captivated both critics and audiences.

"Baby Reindeer" stands out in the limited series category for its innovative approach to storytelling. The series delves into themes of personal trauma, resilience, and redemption, all within a richly layered narrative structure. The plot centers around a central character whose life spirals into chaos after a series of traumatic events. As the story unfolds, viewers are drawn into a complex emotional journey that reveals the character's struggle to regain control and find meaning in their life.

The acclaim for "Baby Reindeer" stems from its ability to blend deep psychological insights with compelling drama. The series combines a gripping plot with strong character development, creating a narrative that is both thought-provoking and engaging. Its success at the Emmys highlights the series' ability to stand out in a competitive field, offering a fresh and impactful take on the limited series format.

Best Actor in a Limited or Anthology Series or Movie: Richard Gadd

Richard Gadd's win for Best Actor in a Limited or Anthology Series or Movie was a defining moment of the 76th Emmys. Gadd's performance in "Baby Reindeer" was nothing short of extraordinary, showcasing his remarkable talent and versatility as an actor. He portrayed the series' protagonist with a depth and authenticity that drew viewers into the character's emotional and psychological struggles.

Gadd's portrayal was marked by its intense emotional range and nuanced delivery. He effectively conveyed the character's vulnerability and inner turmoil, bringing a raw and genuine quality to the role. His performance was instrumental in driving the series' narrative and capturing the audience's empathy and engagement.

The recognition of Gadd's performance at the Emmys was a testament to his skill as an actor and the strength of his role in "Baby Reindeer." His win underscored the importance of powerful, character-driven performances in the limited series genre and celebrated his contribution to the show's success.

Best Actress in a Limited or Anthology Series or Movie: Jodie Foster

Jodie Foster's win for Best Actress in a Limited or Anthology Series or Movie was a highlight of the 76th Emmys. Foster's performance in "Baby

Reindeer" was widely acclaimed for its emotional depth and complexity. As a leading actress, Foster brought a compelling and multidimensional portrayal to her role, adding significant value to the series.

Foster's role in "Baby Reindeer" demanded a nuanced performance, as her character navigated complex emotional terrain and personal challenges. Her portrayal was marked by a profound ability to convey both strength and vulnerability, making her character's journey both relatable and impactful. Foster's skillful execution of her role contributed to the series' success and resonated deeply with viewers.

The Emmys' recognition of Foster's performance celebrated her exceptional talent and the quality of her role in "Baby Reindeer." Her win highlighted the importance of strong female leads in limited series and underscored her status as one of the industry's most accomplished actresses.

Best Supporting Actor in a Limited or Anthology Series or Movie: Lamorne Morris

Lamorne Morris's win for Best Supporting Actor in a Limited or Anthology Series or Movie was a significant achievement for his role in "Baby Reindeer." Morris's performance as a key supporting character added depth and dimension to the series, enhancing its overall narrative and impact.

Morris's portrayal was characterized by its ability to balance both dramatic and subtle comedic elements. His role provided a crucial counterpoint to the central character's journey, offering both support and conflict that enriched the storyline. His performance was marked by its versatility and effectiveness, contributing to the series' success and engaging the audience.

The Emmys' recognition of Morris's performance celebrated his skill as a supporting actor and the strength of his role in "Baby Reindeer." His win underscored the importance of strong supporting performances in enhancing the overall quality of a series and highlighted his contribution to the show's success.

Best Supporting Actress in a Limited or Anthology Series or Movie: Jessica Gunning

Jessica Gunning's win for Best Supporting Actress in a Limited or Anthology Series or Movie was a notable moment at the 76th Emmys. Gunning's performance in "Baby

Reindeer" was praised for its emotional depth and effectiveness in complementing the central narrative. Her role as a supporting character added significant value to the series, enhancing its overall impact.

Gunning's portrayal was marked by its emotional resonance and strong character development. She brought a compelling presence to her role, effectively supporting the central storyline and contributing to the series' thematic richness. Her performance was integral to the narrative, providing both emotional support and depth.

The recognition of Gunning's performance at the Emmys celebrated her talent as a supporting actress and highlighted the importance of strong supporting roles in limited series. Her win underscored the impact of well-crafted performances in enhancing the overall quality and success of a series.

Best Directing for a Limited Series or Anthology Series or Movie: Steven Zaillian

Steven Zaillian's win for Best Directing for a Limited Series or Anthology Series or Movie was a significant accolade at the 76th Emmys. Zaillian's direction of "Baby Reindeer" was instrumental in shaping the series' narrative and visual style, contributing to its critical acclaim and success.

Zaillian's direction was characterized by its meticulous attention to detail and its ability to bring the series' complex story to life. His approach effectively balanced the series' emotional and dramatic elements, creating a cohesive and engaging viewing experience. His skillful direction enhanced the storytelling and allowed the series to achieve its full potential.

The recognition of Zaillian's direction at the Emmys celebrated his contribution to the success of "Baby Reindeer" and highlighted the importance of skilled directing in the limited series format. His win underscored the role of effective direction in shaping the overall quality and impact of a television series.

Analysis of Winning Shows and Performances

The 76th Emmy Awards celebrated a diverse range of achievements in the limited or anthology series category, with "Baby Reindeer" emerging as a standout winner. The series was recognized for its innovative storytelling and exceptional performances, particularly by Richard Gadd and Jodie Foster. Their portrayals brought depth and authenticity to the series, enhancing its overall impact.

The wins for Lamorne Morris and Jessica Gunning highlighted the importance of strong supporting roles in enriching the narrative and adding complexity to the series. Their performances were integral to the success of "Baby Reindeer" and underscored the value of effective supporting roles in limited series.

Steven Zaillian's directing win celebrated his skill in shaping the series' narrative and visual style, contributing to its critical acclaim. The recognition of individual performances and direction in the limited series category reflected the continued evolution of the genre and the importance of well-crafted storytelling and execution.

Overall, the 76th Emmys celebrated a range of achievements in the limited or anthology series category, highlighting the ongoing innovation and talent within the industry. The recognition of "Baby Reindeer" and its cast and crew underscored the series' success and its impact on the limited series genre.

Chapter Six: Variety and Talk Series

Best Scripted Variety Series: Last Week Tonight with John Oliver

At the 76th Emmy Awards, "Last Week Tonight with John Oliver" clinched the accolade for Best Scripted Variety Series, underscoring its continued dominance in the genre. This win solidified the show's reputation for blending insightful political commentary with sharp humor, making it a standout in a competitive field.

"Last Week Tonight with John Oliver," hosted by John Oliver, has established itself as a critical force in scripted variety television. The show's unique format combines deep dives into current events with biting satire, offering viewers both education and entertainment. Its success stems from its ability to address complex issues with clarity and wit, making serious topics accessible and engaging.

Oliver's approach to storytelling carefully researched segments presented with a mix of humor and gravity has resonated with audiences and critics alike. Each episode tackles a specific subject, ranging from political scandals to social justice issues, providing a comprehensive analysis while maintaining a comedic edge. This balance of substance and style is a key reason for the show's acclaim.

The Emmy win for Best Scripted Variety Series acknowledges the show's excellence in blending informative content with entertainment. "Last Week Tonight with John Oliver" continues to push boundaries in the genre, setting a high standard for how scripted variety can address significant issues while captivating audiences.

Best Talk Series: The Daily Show

"The Daily Show" earned the award for Best Talk Series at the 76th Emmys, a testament to its enduring relevance and influence in the landscape of television talk shows. The show, known for its satirical take on current events, has been a staple in American media, shaping public discourse with its unique blend of humor and critique.

Under the stewardship of its various hosts over the years, "The Daily Show" has maintained its position as a leader in talk television. The show's format, which includes interviews, political commentary, and sketches, provides a platform for both entertainment and critical analysis. Its ability to adapt to changing political and social climates while retaining its distinctive voice has been crucial to its longevity and success.

The Emmy win for Best Talk Series celebrates the show's role in influencing public opinion and contributing to political and cultural conversations. "The Daily Show" has become a cultural touchstone, using satire to illuminate issues and provoke thought. This recognition highlights the show's impact and its continued relevance in a rapidly evolving media landscape.

Best Writing for a Variety Special: Alex Edelman: Just for Us

The Emmy for Best Writing for a Variety Special was awarded to "Alex Edelman: Just for Us," acknowledging Edelman's exceptional skill in crafting a compelling and original comedy special. The special, known for its innovative approach and insightful humor, stood out in the variety special category.

"Alex Edelman: Just for Us" showcases Edelman's ability to blend personal anecdotes with broader social commentary, creating a performance that is both entertaining and thought-provoking. His writing skillfully weaves together humor and reflection, offering audiences a unique perspective on contemporary issues. The special's success is attributed to its originality and the depth of Edelman's observations.

The award for Best Writing for a Variety Special highlights the importance of strong writing in creating memorable and impactful comedy. Edelman's win underscores his talent for crafting a narrative that resonates with audiences while maintaining a high level of humor and insight.

Analysis of Winning Shows and Performances

The 76th Emmy Awards celebrated a diverse array of achievements in the variety and talk series categories, with significant wins for "Last Week Tonight with John Oliver," "The Daily Show," and "Alex Edelman: Just for Us." Each of these awards reflects the excellence and innovation present in these genres.

"Last Week Tonight with John Oliver" continues to be a trailblazer in the scripted variety series category, setting a high bar for how television can combine satire and serious journalism. The show's success is a testament to its effective approach to addressing complex issues with both depth and humor. Its Emmy win underscores the importance of engaging and informative content in the variety genre.

"The Daily Show" remains a significant force in the talk series landscape, with its Emmy win highlighting its role in shaping public discourse and providing a platform for critical commentary. The show's ability to adapt and remain relevant demonstrates its enduring appeal and influence. The win acknowledges the show's impact on contemporary media and its contribution to public conversation.

Alex Edelman's "Just for Us" received recognition for its exceptional writing, reflecting the high quality of comedy specials that push the boundaries of the genre. Edelman's ability to blend personal stories with broader commentary illustrates the power of well-crafted humor to engage and provoke thought. The award for Best Writing for a Variety Special celebrates the importance of strong writing in creating impactful and memorable performances.

Overall, the 76th Emmys highlighted the continued evolution and excellence within the variety and talk series genres. The recognition of these shows and performances reflects the dynamic nature of television and the ongoing innovation in delivering content that informs, entertains, and resonates with audiences.

Chapter Seven: Reality and Competition Shows

Best Reality Competition Program: The Traitors

At the 76th Emmy Awards, "The Traitors" emerged as the winner of the Best Reality Competition Program, marking a significant achievement in the realm of reality television. This victory underscores the show's unique appeal and its ability to captivate audiences with its innovative format and engaging content.

"The Traitors" has garnered acclaim for its fresh approach to the reality competition genre. Unlike traditional reality shows that often revolve around physical challenges or social dynamics alone, "The Traitors" combines elements of strategic deception, psychological intrigue, and interpersonal drama. The show's format involves contestants working together to complete challenges while simultaneously trying to identify and eliminate "traitors" within their midst. This mix of teamwork, betrayal, and strategy creates a compelling narrative that keeps viewers on the edge of their seats.

The show's success can be attributed to several key factors. First, the unique format of "The Traitors" introduces an element of suspense that is often lacking in other reality competition programs. The constant tension between contestants, coupled with the strategic gameplay of identifying traitors, provides a dynamic and engaging viewing experience. This tension is further amplified by the show's well-crafted challenges and intricate plot twists, which keep both contestants and viewers guessing.

Additionally, the casting of "The Traitors" has been crucial to its success. The show features a diverse group of contestants with varying backgrounds, personalities, and strategies. This diversity not only adds depth to the show but also ensures a range of interactions and conflicts that enhance the overall drama. The contestants' varying approaches to gameplay whether through alliances, deceit, or outright confrontation—create a rich tapestry of interactions that drive the narrative forward.

The win for Best Reality Competition Program reflects the show's ability to innovate within the genre and offer something new to audiences. By blending elements of psychological thriller with reality competition, "The Traitors" has set a new standard for what a reality competition show can be. The Emmy win is a testament to the show's effectiveness in engaging viewers and creating a memorable viewing experience.

Analysis of Winning Shows and Performances

The success of "The Traitors" at the 76th Emmy Awards highlights a broader trend in reality and competition shows: the increasing emphasis on strategic gameplay, psychological dynamics, and unique formats. This shift reflects a growing appetite among audiences for reality television that goes beyond traditional formats and offers a deeper, more engaging experience.

Innovative Formats and Viewer Engagement

One of the key reasons for "The Traitors" success is its innovative format. The show's blend of strategic deception and psychological intrigue introduces a new layer of complexity to the reality competition genre. By focusing on the psychological aspects of gameplay—such as the challenge of identifying traitors and the strategies involved in navigating alliances—the show creates a highly engaging viewing experience. This format not only captures the interest of viewers but also encourages them to actively participate in the game, as they try to predict the outcomes and identify the traitors themselves.

The success of "The Traitors" also reflects a broader trend in reality television, where unique and unconventional formats are becoming increasingly popular. Shows that offer fresh perspectives and innovative twists on traditional formats are more likely to stand out and capture the attention of both viewers and critics. This trend is evident in the growing number of reality competition programs that focus on strategic gameplay, psychological drama, and complex narratives, rather than just physical challenges or superficial interactions.

Diverse Casting and Rich Narratives

Another significant factor in the success of "The Traitors" is its diverse casting and the rich narratives that emerge from the contestants' interactions. The show features a wide range of personalities and backgrounds, which adds depth to the competition and enhances the overall drama. The contestants' different approaches to gameplay—whether through strategic alliances, deception, or confrontation—create a dynamic and multifaceted narrative that keeps viewers engaged.

The diversity of the cast also contributes to the show's appeal by offering a variety of perspectives and experiences. This diversity not only enriches the storytelling but also ensures that the show resonates with a broad audience. By showcasing a range of personalities and strategies, "The Traitors" provides a more nuanced and relatable viewing experience, allowing viewers to connect with the contestants and become invested in their journeys.

Strategic Gameplay and Psychological Depth

The emphasis on strategic gameplay and psychological depth is another key factor in the success of "The Traitors." The show's format challenges contestants to navigate complex social dynamics and engage in strategic deception, creating a rich and engaging narrative. This focus on strategy and psychology adds a layer of sophistication to the competition, setting it apart from other reality shows that may rely more heavily on physical challenges or superficial drama.

The psychological aspect of the show such as the tension between contestants trying to identify the traitors and the strategies employed to achieve this—creates a compelling and immersive experience. This depth of gameplay not only keeps viewers intrigued but also allows them to engage more deeply with the show's narrative. By focusing on the psychological elements of competition, "The Traitors" offers a more intellectually stimulating and engaging viewing experience.

Impact on the Reality Television Landscape

The success of "The Traitors" at the Emmys represents a significant shift in the reality television landscape. The show's innovative format and emphasis on strategic gameplay reflect a growing trend towards more sophisticated and engaging reality programming. As audiences continue to seek out fresh and unique content, reality television producers are likely to explore new formats and approaches that offer greater depth and complexity.

"The Traitors" serves as a prime example of how reality competition shows can evolve to meet the changing demands of viewers. By incorporating elements of psychological intrigue, strategic gameplay, and diverse casting, the show has set a new standard for the genre. Its Emmy win is a testament to the effectiveness of this approach and a reflection of the evolving landscape of reality television.

In conclusion, the recognition of "The Traitors" as Best Reality Competition Program at the 76th Emmys highlights the show's success in innovating within the genre and offering a unique and engaging viewing experience. The show's innovative format, diverse casting, and emphasis on strategic gameplay and psychological depth have set it apart from other reality competition programs, making it a standout in the field. As reality television continues to evolve, "The Traitors" serves as a powerful example of how new formats and approaches can capture the imagination of audiences and achieve critical acclaim.

Chapter Eight: Writing and Directing

The 76th Emmy Awards highlighted some remarkable achievements in writing and directing, celebrating the creative talents behind some of the most compelling television of the year. The winners in these categories included writers and directors who have pushed the boundaries of their craft, resulting in unforgettable television moments and groundbreaking series. This section delves into the accomplishments of the winners in key writing and directing categories, and analyzes the impact of their contributions.

Best Writing for a Drama Series: Will Smith

Will Smith, acclaimed for his multifaceted career as an actor and producer, made a significant mark in the world of television writing with his work on a standout drama series. His win for Best Writing for a Drama Series is a testament to his ability to craft compelling narratives and complex characters that resonate with audiences.

Smith's writing in this category demonstrated a deep understanding of character development and thematic exploration. His work often delves into nuanced portrayals of personal and societal conflicts, reflecting a keen insight into human nature and contemporary issues. The drama series he wrote for brought to life a story that was both emotionally gripping and intellectually stimulating, engaging viewers with its depth and sophistication.

Smith's success in this category underscores the importance of strong writing in television. His ability to blend poignant storytelling with intricate plotlines has not only captivated audiences but also set a high standard for drama series writing. The win reflects his skill in creating narratives that are both powerful and thought-provoking, solidifying his reputation as a leading writer in the industry.

Best Writing for a Limited or Anthology Series or Movie: Richard Gadd

Richard Gadd's achievement in winning Best Writing for a Limited or Anthology Series or Movie highlights his exceptional talent in crafting self-contained stories with significant emotional and narrative impact. His work in this category showcased his ability to create compelling, standalone narratives that captivate and engage viewers from beginning to end.

Gadd's writing often involves a deep exploration of characters and themes, offering a fresh and original perspective on various subjects. His limited or anthology series or movie demonstrated a mastery of storytelling, with well-developed characters and intricate plotlines that left a lasting impression on audiences. His work is characterized by its originality and emotional depth, making it stand out in a competitive field.

The recognition of Gadd's writing underscores the importance of strong narrative structure and character development in limited series and movies. His ability to craft a complete and impactful story in a condensed format speaks to his skill as a writer and his ability to deliver powerful and memorable television experiences.

Best Writing for a Comedy Series: Lucia Aniello, Paul W. Downs, Jen Statsky

The team of Lucia Aniello, Paul W. Downs, and Jen Statsky was honored with Best Writing for a Comedy Series, reflecting their exceptional collaborative effort in crafting a series that is both hilarious and insightful. Their work exemplifies the essence of great comedy writing, blending sharp wit with clever storytelling to create a show that resonates with audiences.

Aniello, Downs, and Statsky's writing is characterized by its originality and humor, with each episode delivering a fresh perspective on relatable themes and situations. Their ability to balance comedy with emotional depth adds layers to their characters and stories, making the series not only funny but also meaningful. The team's work demonstrates a keen understanding of comedic timing and narrative structure, contributing to the show's success and its ability to engage viewers.

The win for Best Writing for a Comedy Series highlights the impact of well-crafted comedy on audiences. The trio's ability to create memorable and engaging content reflects their talent and dedication to the craft of writing. Their success underscores the importance of innovation and creativity in comedy writing, setting a high bar for future entries in the genre.

Best Directing for a Drama Series: Frederick E.O. Toye

Frederick E.O. Toye's recognition for Best Directing for a Drama Series highlights his skill in bringing complex narratives and characters to life with visual and emotional depth. Toye's direction in the drama series demonstrated a masterful control of tone, pacing, and character development, contributing significantly to the series' success.

Toye's approach to directing involves a meticulous attention to detail and a deep understanding of the narrative. His ability to guide actors through emotionally charged scenes and to craft visually striking compositions enhances the storytelling and immerses viewers in the drama. His direction often involves creating a nuanced atmosphere that complements the writing, making the series not only engaging but also visually captivating.

The award for Best Directing for a Drama Series underscores the importance of a director's role in shaping the final product. Toye's success reflects his ability to elevate the material and create a cohesive and impactful viewing experience. His work exemplifies the critical role of direction in the success of a drama series.

Best Directing for a Limited Series or Anthology Series or Movie: Steven Zaillian

Steven Zaillian's win for Best Directing for a Limited Series or Anthology Series or Movie highlights his exceptional talent in directing complex and compelling standalone narratives. Zaillian's work in this category demonstrated a deep understanding of storytelling and a keen eye for visual and emotional detail.

Zaillian's direction is characterized by its precision and sensitivity, creating a strong connection between the narrative and the audience. His ability to handle intricate plots and develop characters within a limited timeframe speaks to his skill and experience as a director. The limited or anthology series or movie he directed showcased his talent for crafting engaging and impactful stories that resonate with viewers.

The recognition of Zaillian's directing emphasizes the importance of strong direction in limited and anthology formats. His success reflects his ability to deliver a powerful and cohesive narrative within a condensed format, setting a high standard for future entries in the category.

Best Directing for a Comedy Series: Christopher Storer

Christopher Storer's achievement in winning Best Directing for a Comedy Series highlights his skill in creating a visually and narratively engaging comedy. Storer's direction in the comedy series demonstrated a deep understanding of comedic timing, character dynamics, and visual storytelling.

Storer's approach to directing involves a careful balance of humor and heart, creating a series that is both entertaining and emotionally resonant. His ability to guide performances and craft visual compositions that enhance the comedic elements of the show contributes to its overall success. Storer's direction ensures that each episode delivers a cohesive and engaging experience, keeping viewers entertained and invested in the characters and story.

The award for Best Directing for a Comedy Series underscores the impact of effective direction on the success of a comedy. Storer's work exemplifies the importance of visual and narrative coherence in creating memorable and engaging comedy.

Analysis of Winning Writers and Directors

The recognition of these writers and directors at the 76th Emmy Awards highlights several key aspects of successful television writing and directing.

1. Innovation and Originality: Each winner has demonstrated a unique approach to their craft, whether through innovative storytelling, fresh

comedic perspectives, or nuanced drama. The emphasis on originality and creativity reflects a broader trend in television towards more diverse and compelling content.

2. Emotional and Narrative Depth: The ability to create emotionally resonant and narratively rich content is a common thread among the winners. Their work showcases a deep understanding of character development, thematic exploration, and storytelling, contributing to their success in their respective categories.

3. Collaborative Efforts: Many of the winners, particularly in writing categories, have achieved success through collaborative efforts. The teamwork of writers and directors often leads to a more refined and impactful final product,

highlighting the importance of collaboration in the creative process.

4. Visual and Emotional Impact: Directors like Frederick E.O. Toye and Steven Zaillian have demonstrated the importance of visual storytelling and emotional depth. Their ability to create immersive and impactful experiences underscores the critical role of direction in shaping the final product.

In conclusion, the achievements of these writers and directors at the 76th Emmys reflect their exceptional talent and contributions to the television industry. Their work sets a high standard for writing and directing, showcasing the importance of innovation, emotional depth, and effective collaboration in creating compelling and memorable television.

Chapter Nine: Notable Nominations and Snubs

The 76th Emmy Awards celebrated outstanding achievements in television, but as with every awards ceremony, the nominations and outcomes generated plenty of discussion. While some shows and individuals were recognized for their exceptional work, others faced surprising snubs that sparked conversations among critics and fans alike. This section examines the notable nominations and surprises, as well as the noteworthy snubs and missed opportunities of the 76th Emmys.

Top Nominations and Surprises

The 76th Emmys were marked by a mix of anticipated wins and unexpected recognitions.

Certain nominations stood out for their significance, while others surprised both industry insiders and audiences.

1. Breakthrough Nominations:

-"Shogun" and "Baby Reindeer": One of the most talked-about surprises was the prominence of "Shogun" and "Baby Reindeer" in the nominations. Both series, though critically acclaimed, were considered underdogs in their respective categories. "Shogun" impressed with its dramatic storytelling and compelling performances, leading to multiple nominations including Best Drama Series and individual nods for Hiroyuki Sanada and Anna Sawai. Similarly, "Baby Reindeer" made a notable impact in the Limited or Anthology Series categories, garnering attention for its innovative narrative and powerful performances.

-"The Traitors" in Reality Competition: Another surprise was "The Traitors" securing the Best Reality Competition Program award. The series, which offered a unique blend of strategy and reality television, outperformed established favorites and captured the Emmy for its inventive approach and engaging content.

2. Unexpected Wins:

-"Hacks" for Comedy Series: While "Hacks" had already established itself as a strong contender, its sweeping victory in the Comedy Series category was testament to the series' exceptional writing and performances. The recognition of Jean Smart for Best Actress and Jeremy Allen White for Best Actor further highlighted the show's widespread acclaim and its ability to stand out in a competitive field.

-Christopher Storer for Comedy Series Direction: The award for Best Directing in a Comedy Series going to Christopher Storer was notable. His direction of "Hacks" was praised for its seamless blend of humor and emotional depth, contributing significantly to the show's success.

3. Recognition of Lesser-Known Projects:

-"Last Week Tonight with John Oliver" for Scripted Variety Series: The continued success of "Last Week Tonight with John Oliver" in the Scripted Variety Series category was noteworthy. Despite the intense competition from other talk and variety shows, John Oliver's ability to blend humor with insightful commentary ensured the series maintained its strong presence in the Emmys.

-"Alex Edelman: Just for Us" for Writing: Alex Edelman's win for Best Writing in a Variety Special was a notable achievement. His unique blend of personal storytelling and comedy resonated with both the audience and critics, showcasing the impact of fresh and original voices in the variety space.

Noteworthy Snubs and Missed Opportunities

While the Emmys celebrated many deserving winners, several notable snubs and missed opportunities generated significant discussion. These omissions highlight the subjective nature of awards and the ever-present debates over which shows and individuals were overlooked.

1. Major Snubs:

-"Succession" for Drama Series: Despite being a critical darling and a favorite in various awards circuits, "Succession" did not secure the Best Drama Series award. The show's intricate storytelling and powerful performances were widely praised, making its exclusion from the top honor a surprising decision.

-"The Bear" in Key Categories: "The Bear," a series that received considerable acclaim for its raw depiction of the culinary world and its intense performances, was expected to be a major player at the Emmys. However, it was notably absent in several key categories, including Best Drama Series and major acting awards, leaving many fans and critics questioning the oversight.

2. Missed Opportunities for Individual Performances:

-Acting Nominations for "The Bear": Many felt that the cast of "The Bear," including standout performances by Jeremy Allen White, were deserving of more recognition. The absence of nominations for key performances in the series was seen as a missed opportunity to honor exceptional acting talent.

-Jodie Foster for "Baby Reindeer": Jodie Foster's performance in "Baby Reindeer" was highly acclaimed, yet she was overlooked for a Best Actress nomination. This omission was particularly surprising given the critical praise she received for her role, leading to discussions about the criteria and considerations involved in the nomination process.

3. Criticisms of the Selection Process:

-Focus on Mainstream Shows: Some critics argued that the Emmys' focus on mainstream and high-profile shows resulted in the exclusion of smaller, yet highly deserving projects. This sentiment was echoed in the case of several indie and lesser-known series that failed to receive recognition despite their strong performances and innovative content.

-Inconsistent Recognition Across Categories: The Emmys were also criticized for their inconsistent recognition across different categories. For instance, while certain shows received multiple nominations, they were overlooked in key categories where their excellence was evident. This inconsistency led to debates about the fairness and comprehensiveness of the selection process.

In conclusion, the 76th Emmys offered a blend of expected victories and surprising outcomes, reflecting the dynamic nature of television and the awards process. The notable nominations and surprises showcased the diversity and creativity in the industry, while the snubs and missed opportunities underscored the challenges and debates inherent in award selections. As always, the Emmys serve as a snapshot of the television landscape, celebrating achievements while also highlighting the subjectivity and unpredictability of recognizing excellence in entertainment.

Chapter Ten: Industry Impact

The 76th Emmy Awards provided a significant moment for reflection and change within the television industry. As the industry's most prestigious awards, the Emmys often serve as a barometer for trends, tastes, and the evolving nature of television. This year's awards not only celebrated outstanding achievements but also had far-reaching implications for television trends and the industry's future. This section delves into how the 76th Emmys shaped television trends and the long-term implications for the industry.

How the 76th Emmys Shaped Television Trends

The 76th Emmys highlighted several emerging trends in television, reflecting broader shifts in viewer preferences, content production, and distribution strategies.

1. Diversity and Inclusion:

-Broadening Representation: One of the most notable trends was the emphasis on diversity and inclusion. This year's winners and nominees showcased a broad spectrum of voices and stories, reflecting a growing industry commitment to representing different cultures, identities, and experiences. For example, "Shogun," which features a predominantly Asian cast and explores historical themes from a non-Western perspective, demonstrated the increasing appetite for diverse narratives. Similarly, "Baby Reindeer" highlighted the importance of unique voices and stories that break away from traditional norms.

-Impact on Future Productions: This focus on diversity is likely to influence future content creation, pushing studios and networks to prioritize inclusive storytelling and representation both in front of and behind the camera. The awards' recognition of diverse projects could encourage more creators to explore and produce content that reflects a wider array of experiences and backgrounds.

2. Streaming and Digital Platforms:

-Rise of Streaming Platforms: The dominance of streaming platforms was evident in the nominations and wins at the 76th Emmys. Shows like "Baby Reindeer," which aired on streaming services, were recognized alongside traditional network and cable productions. This trend underscores the growing influence of streaming platforms in shaping television content and audience engagement.

- Shifting Viewing Habits: The success of streaming-based shows reflects a shift in viewing habits, with audiences increasingly turning to digital platforms for high-quality, innovative content. This shift is likely to drive further investment in streaming content and encourage traditional networks to adapt to changing viewer preferences.

3. Genre Innovation:

-Blending Genres: The Emmys showcased a trend towards genre innovation, with several winning shows blending elements from different genres to create unique and engaging content.

For instance, "The Bear" combined drama with elements of reality television to offer a fresh perspective on the culinary world. Similarly, "The Traitors" brought a novel twist to the reality competition genre, incorporating elements of strategy and suspense.

-Encouraging Creativity: This genre-blending trend encourages creators to experiment with new formats and storytelling techniques, potentially leading to more diverse and inventive programming. The recognition of such innovative content at the Emmys may inspire other creators to push the boundaries of traditional genre conventions.

4. Focus on High-Quality Writing and Direction:

-Elevating Craftsmanship: The awards highlighted the critical role of exceptional writing and direction in achieving critical success. Winners like Christopher Storer for Best Directing in a Comedy Series and Will Smith for Best Writing in a Drama Series exemplify the importance of strong craftsmanship in television. This focus on writing and directing excellence underscores the need for high-quality storytelling and creative vision in producing standout content.

-Influencing Industry Standards: As the industry recognizes and rewards outstanding writing and direction, it may set new standards for television production. Creators and studios might place greater emphasis on these aspects, leading to a higher overall quality of content across the board.

Long-Term Implications for the Industry

The outcomes of the 76th Emmys are likely to have lasting effects on the television industry, shaping its trajectory in several key areas.

1. Increased Investment in Diverse Content:

-Encouraging Investment: The success of diverse and inclusive programming at the Emmys is expected to encourage greater investment in such content. Networks and streaming platforms may prioritize projects that reflect a range of perspectives and stories, leading to a more inclusive and representative television landscape.

- Cultural Impact: This shift has the potential to create a more culturally rich and varied television environment, fostering a greater understanding and appreciation of different cultures and experiences. As a result, viewers may see more stories that resonate with a broader audience, contributing to a more inclusive media landscape.

2. Strengthening the Role of Streaming Platforms:

-Increased Competition: The prominence of streaming platforms at the Emmys suggests a strengthening of their role in the television industry. As these platforms continue to gain recognition, traditional networks may face increased competition, prompting them to innovate and adapt to stay relevant.

-Evolving Distribution Models: The success of streaming-based content may lead to further changes in distribution models, with more emphasis on digital platforms and on-demand viewing. This shift could alter how content is produced, marketed, and consumed, influencing industry practices and audience expectations.

3. Emphasis on Innovation and Creativity:

-Encouraging New Ideas: The recognition of genre-blending and innovative content at the Emmys is likely to encourage creators to explore new ideas and formats. This emphasis on creativity may lead to the development of unique and original programming, pushing the boundaries of traditional television and offering fresh experiences for viewers.

-Setting New Industry Standards: As the industry rewards innovation, it may set new benchmarks for content creation and storytelling. Creators and studios might be inspired to elevate their craft and take creative risks, leading to a more dynamic and evolving television landscape.

4. Shaping Future Talent Development:

-Attracting Emerging Talent: The success of lesser-known projects and emerging voices at the Emmys could attract new talent to the industry. As more opportunities arise for diverse and innovative creators, the industry may see an influx of fresh perspectives and voices, enriching the overall creative ecosystem.

-Fostering New Generations: The recognition of outstanding writing, directing, and acting may also inspire the next generation of television professionals. Aspiring creators and performers may be motivated by the achievements of their peers, leading to a new wave of talent that continues to shape the future of television.

In summary, the 76th Emmy Awards have had a profound impact on the television industry, influencing trends, shaping viewer preferences, and setting new standards for content creation. The emphasis on diversity, streaming platforms, genre innovation, and high-quality craftsmanship reflects a dynamic and evolving landscape, with lasting implications for the industry's future. As television continues to adapt and grow, the effects of this year's Emmys are likely to resonate for years to come, shaping the direction and development of television content and production.

Chapter Eleven – The Governors Award

The Governors Award, a distinguished honor presented by the Academy of Television Arts & Sciences, is among the highest accolades in the television industry. This award recognizes outstanding contributions to the television industry that transcend traditional categories and have made a significant impact on the field. The 76th Emmy Awards provided a notable occasion for this prestigious award, celebrating the remarkable achievements of Greg Berlanti, whose contributions to television have reshaped the landscape of the medium. This section delves into the presentation and significance of the Governors Award and explores Greg Berlanti's exceptional impact on television.

Presentation and Significance of the Award

1. Historical Context and Purpose:

-Origins of the Governors Award: The Governors Award was established by the Academy of Television Arts & Sciences to honor individuals or organizations that have made exceptional contributions to the television industry. Unlike other Emmys, which recognize achievements in specific categories such as acting, writing, or directing, the Governors Award is given for a lifetime of work or a singular, transformative impact on the industry.

-Purpose and Prestige: The purpose of the Governors Award is to acknowledge those who have demonstrated an enduring commitment to excellence and innovation in television. This award holds a special place in the Emmys as it honors achievements that may not fit into traditional award categories but have nonetheless made a profound impact on the industry. The presentation of this award is a moment of celebration and reflection on the broader contributions of the honoree.

2. Presentation at the 76th Emmys:

- Ceremonial Moment:At the 76th Emmy Awards, the Governors Award was presented with great ceremony and recognition. The presentation typically involves a special segment dedicated to highlighting the achievements of the recipient, accompanied by tributes from colleagues, industry leaders, and peers. This year's presentation was marked by an emphasis on Greg Berlanti's transformative influence on television.

-Tributes and Acknowledgments: During the award presentation, a series of tributes and video montages showcased Berlanti's extensive body of work and his impact on the industry. Colleagues, collaborators, and industry veterans spoke about his contributions, highlighting the breadth and depth of his influence on modern television.

3. Significance for the Television Industry:

-Recognizing Innovation: The Governors Award serves as a testament to the recipient's innovative spirit and contributions to the evolution of television. By honoring individuals who have made groundbreaking advancements or created influential content, the award acknowledges the role of visionary creators in shaping the medium.

-Inspiring Future Generations: The recognition of exceptional individuals through the Governors Award also serves to inspire future generations of television professionals. It underscores the potential for creativity, dedication, and innovation to make a lasting impact on the industry. The award highlights the importance of pursuing excellence and contributing meaningfully to the field.

Greg Berlanti's Contribution and Impact

1. Overview of Greg Berlanti's Career:

-Early Beginnings:Greg Berlanti began his career as a writer and producer, quickly establishing himself as a prominent figure in the television industry. His early work included notable contributions to series like "Dawson's

Creek" and "Everwood," where his storytelling skills and creative vision began to shine.

- Expanding Influence: Berlanti's influence expanded significantly with the creation and production of successful television series, including "Arrow," "The Flash," "Supergirl," and "Riverdale." His ability to craft compelling narratives and develop diverse, engaging characters has earned him acclaim and a dedicated following.

2. Innovation in Television:

-Revitalizing the Superhero Genre: One of Berlanti's most notable contributions has been his revitalization of the superhero genre on television. Through the creation of the Arrowverse, Berlanti brought a fresh and interconnected approach to superhero storytelling, which has influenced how such narratives are presented across various media platforms.

-Diverse Storytelling: Berlanti's work is characterized by its emphasis on diversity and representation. Series like "Love, Simon" and "You" have explored a wide range of themes, including LGBTQ+ representation, mental health, and social issues. This focus on inclusive storytelling has resonated with audiences and set new standards for representation in television.

3. Impact on Industry Practices:

-Shaping Television Landscapes: Berlanti's impact extends beyond individual shows; he has played a crucial role in shaping the broader television landscape. His approach to serialized storytelling, character development, and cross-platform narratives has influenced other creators and set trends within the industry.

-Mentorship and Collaboration: Berlanti's influence also extends to his role as a mentor and collaborator. He has worked with a diverse array of talent and fostered an environment of creativity and innovation. His ability to collaborate effectively and nurture emerging talent has contributed to the growth and evolution of the television industry.

4. Long-Term Legacy:

-Enduring Influence: Berlanti's contributions have had a lasting impact on television, with his work continuing to influence new projects and creators. His innovative approach to storytelling and commitment to diverse representation have set a high bar for future television content.

-Inspiring Change: The recognition of Greg Berlanti through the Governors Award underscores the importance of creativity, innovation, and dedication in television. His achievements serve as a source of inspiration for others in the industry, demonstrating how visionary work can drive progress and shape the future of television.

In summary, the Governors Award presented at the 76th Emmys celebrated the exceptional contributions of Greg Berlanti, highlighting his transformative impact on the television industry. Through his innovative storytelling, commitment to diversity, and influence on industry practices, Berlanti has made a profound and lasting impact on television. The award not only honors his achievements but also serves as a testament to the broader significance of excellence and innovation in the medium.

Conclusion

As the 76th Emmy Awards come to a close, it provides an opportune moment to reflect on the highlights and implications of this year's event. The Emmy Awards, held annually, celebrate the finest achievements in television, and the 76th iteration was no exception. This conclusion aims to summarize the key takeaways from the ceremony and offer reflections on its broader significance.

Summary of Key Takeaways

1. Historic Wins and Achievements:
The 76th Emmy Awards were marked by several historic wins and notable achievements across various categories. Disney emerged as a dominant force, breaking records with its

numerous accolades. This year, Disney's unprecedented success highlighted the company's significant impact on the television landscape, reinforcing its position as a powerhouse in entertainment.

One of the standout achievements was "The Bear," which made history with its wins, showcasing the show's exceptional storytelling and performances. The series not only garnered widespread acclaim but also set new standards for what can be achieved in the drama genre. Similarly, "Shogun" made headlines with its groundbreaking awards, signaling a shift in television trends and audience preferences.

In the realm of limited or anthology series, "Baby Reindeer" emerged as a major winner, reflecting the growing appreciation for unique and compelling narratives in this category. The recognition of such diverse and innovative content underscores the Emmys' role in celebrating the breadth of storytelling in television.

2. Exceptional Performances:

The awards also celebrated outstanding individual performances. Hiroyuki Sanada and Anna Sawai took home the awards for Best Actor and Best Actress in a Drama Series, respectively, reflecting their remarkable contributions to "Shogun." Their performances were pivotal in defining the show's success and resonated strongly with both critics and audiences.

In the comedy category, Jeremy Allen White and Jean Smart were honored as Best Actor and Best Actress, highlighting their exceptional work in "Hacks." Their performances contributed significantly to the show's acclaim and demonstrated the importance of strong, nuanced portrayals in comedy.

The Limited or Anthology Series category saw Richard Gadd and Jodie Foster recognized for their roles in "Baby Reindeer," further emphasizing the impact of individual talent on the success of a series. The recognition of their performances reinforces the value of compelling storytelling and strong character portrayals in this genre.

3. Innovation and Industry Trends:

The 76th Emmys also reflected broader industry trends, including a growing emphasis on diversity and innovative storytelling. The success of shows like "The Bear" and "Baby Reindeer" signifies a shift towards more varied and inclusive narratives. This year's winners demonstrated a commitment to exploring diverse themes and pushing the boundaries of traditional television storytelling.

The recognition of Greg Berlanti with the Governors Award underscored the importance of innovation and visionary contributions in shaping the future of television. Berlanti's impact on the industry, particularly through his work in the superhero genre and commitment to diverse representation, highlights the evolving landscape of television and the role of influential creators in driving change.

Reflections on the 76th Emmy Awards

1. Celebration of Excellence:

The 76th Emmy Awards served as a celebration of excellence in television, bringing together industry professionals to recognize and honor the best in the field. The ceremony highlighted the achievements of individuals and shows that have made a significant impact over the past year, showcasing the talent and creativity that drive the industry forward.

The awards also provided a platform for celebrating the diverse range of content available on television today. From groundbreaking dramas to innovative comedies and compelling limited series, the Emmys highlighted the richness and variety of television programming. This celebration of excellence reinforces the importance of recognizing and supporting high-quality content in the industry.

2. Reflecting on Industry Changes:
The 76th Emmys also offered insights into the ongoing changes and trends within the television industry. The emphasis on diverse storytelling,

the success of new and innovative shows, and the recognition of emerging talent all reflect the dynamic nature of the industry. As television continues to evolve, the Emmys serve as a barometer for these changes, highlighting shifts in audience preferences and industry practices.

The recognition of new and groundbreaking content also signals a broader trend towards embracing unconventional narratives and exploring underrepresented themes. This shift aligns with the growing demand for more inclusive and diverse storytelling, which is increasingly reflected in the content celebrated by the Emmys.

3. Looking Ahead:

As the 76th Emmy Awards conclude, the industry looks ahead to future trends and developments. The success of this year's winners and the celebration of innovative content set a precedent for what can be achieved in television. The Emmys continue to play a crucial role in shaping the direction of the industry, and the recognition of outstanding work serves as both a reflection of current trends and a catalyst for future innovation.

In summary, the 76th Emmy Awards highlighted the achievements and contributions of individuals and shows that have made a significant impact on the television industry. The celebration of excellence, the reflection on industry changes, and the anticipation of future trends all underscore the importance of recognizing and supporting high-quality content. As the industry continues to evolve, the Emmys will remain a key platform for celebrating the best in television and driving progress within the field.

Appendices

Full List of Winners and Nominees

1. Drama Series

    A) Best Drama Series:

- Winner: Shogun

- Nominees:

    - Succession

    - The Crown

    - Better Call Saul

    - The White Lotus

    - Yellowjackets

    B) Best Actor in a Drama Series:

- Winner: Hiroyuki Sanada (Shogun)

- Nominees:

    - Jeremy Strong (Succession)

    - Brian Cox (Succession)

- Bob Odenkirk (Better Call Saul)

- Adam Driver (The Crown)

- Matthew Macfadyen (Succession)

C) Best Actress in a Drama Series:

- Winner: Anna Sawai (Shogun)

- Nominees:

- Olivia Colman (The Crown)

- Sarah Snook (Succession)

- Jennifer Coolidge (The White Lotus)

- Jodie Comer (Killing Eve)

- Melanie Lynskey (Yellowjackets)

D) Best Supporting Actor in a Drama Series:

- Winner: Billy Crudup (The Morning Show)

- Nominees:

- Nicholas Braun (Succession)

- Kieran Culkin (Succession)

- Matthew Macfadyen (Succession)

- John Lithgow (The Crown)

- Jonathan Banks (Better Call Saul)

E) Best Supporting Actress in a Drama Series:

- Winner: Elizabeth Debicki (The Crown)

- Nominees:

  - Julia Garner (Ozark)

  - Rhea Seehorn (Better Call Saul)

  - Sarah Snook (Succession)

  - Sydney Sweeney (Euphoria)

  - Thuso Mbedu (The Underground Railroad)

F) Best Directing for a Drama Series:

- Winner: Frederick E.O. Toye (Shogun)

- Nominees:

  - Adam McKay (Succession)

  - Sam Levinson (Euphoria)

- David Frankel (The Morning Show)

- Jessica Yu (The White Lotus)

- Scott Frank (The Queen's Gambit)

2. Comedy Series

A) Best Comedy Series:

- Winner: Hacks

- Nominees:

  - Ted Lasso

  - The Marvelous Mrs. Maisel

  - Barry

  - Brooklyn Nine-Nine

  - Mythic Quest: Raven's Banquet

B) Best Actor in a Comedy Series:

- Winner: Jeremy Allen White (The Bear)

- Nominees:

  - Jason Sudeikis (Ted Lasso)

- Bill Hader (Barry)

- Donald Glover (Atlanta)

- Steve Martin (Only Murders in the Building)

- Martin Short (Only Murders in the Building)

C) Best Actress in a Comedy Series:

- Winner: Jean Smart (Hacks)

- Nominees:

- Rachel Brosnahan (The Marvelous Mrs. Maisel)

- Quinta Brunson (Abbott Elementary)

- Issa Rae (Insecure)

- Pamela Adlon (Better Things)

- Kaley Cuoco (The Flight Attendant)

D) Best Supporting Actor in a Comedy Series:

- Winner: Ebon Moss-Bachrach (The Bear)
- Nominees:
  - Brett Goldstein (Ted Lasso)
  - Henry Winkler (Barry)
  - Tony Shalhoub (The Marvelous Mrs. Maisel)
  - Adam Shulman (Mythic Quest: Raven's Banquet)
  - Ayo Edebiri (The Bear)

E) Best Supporting Actress in a Comedy Series:
- Winner: Liza Colón-Zayas (Hacks)
- Nominees:
  - Hannah Einbinder (Hacks)
  - Janelle James (Abbott Elementary)
  - Sharon Horgan (Bad Sisters)
  - Rita Moreno (One Day at a Time)
  - Laurie Metcalf (The Conners)

F) Best Directing for a Comedy Series:
- Winner: Christopher Storer (The Bear)
- Nominees:
  - Mike White (The White Lotus)
  - Bill Hader (Barry)
  - Amy Sherman-Palladino (The Marvelous Mrs. Maisel)
  - Andrew Cividino (Schitt's Creek)
  - Schitt's Creek (Daniel Levy)

3. Limited or Anthology Series

A) Best Limited or Anthology Series:
- Winner: Baby Reindeer
- Nominees:
  - Dahmer – Monster: The Jeffrey Dahmer Story
  - The White Lotus: Sicily

- The Bear

- Pam & Tommy

- Inventing Anna

B) Best Actor in a Limited or Anthology Series or Movie:

- Winner: Richard Gadd (Baby Reindeer)
- Nominees:

    - Evan Peters (Dahmer – Monster: The Jeffrey Dahmer Story)

    - Sebastian Stan (Pam & Tommy)

    - Jeremy Renner (Mayor of Kingstown)

    - Eddie Redmayne (The Good Nurse)

    - Daniel Radcliffe (Weird: The Al Yankovic Story)

C)   Best Actress in a Limited or Anthology Series or Movie:

- Winner: Jodie Foster (Baby Reindeer)

- Nominees:

  - Lily James (Pam & Tommy)

  - Julia Garner (Inventing Anna)

  - Amanda Seyfried (The Dropout)

  - Jessica Chastain (George & Tammy)

  - Emily Blunt (The English)

D) Best Supporting Actor in a Limited or Anthology Series or Movie:

- Winner: Lamorne Morris (Baby Reindeer)
- Nominees:

  - Richard Jenkins (Dahmer – Monster: The Jeffrey Dahmer Story)

  - Seth Rogen (Pam & Tommy)

  - Paul Walter Hauser (Black Bird)

  - Ncuti Gatwa (The Woman in the House Across the Street from the Girl in the Window)

  - F. Murray Abraham (The White Lotus: Sicily)

F) Best Supporting Actress in a Limited or Anthology Series or Movie:

- Winner: Jessica Gunning (Baby Reindeer)
- Nominees:

  - Niecy Nash (Dahmer – Monster: The Jeffrey Dahmer Story)

  - Toni Collette (The Staircase)

  - Aubrey Plaza (The White Lotus: Sicily)

  - Angela Bassett (The Good Nurse)

  - Dominique Fishback (Swarm)

G) Best Directing for a Limited Series or Anthology Series or Movie:

- Winner: Steven Zaillian (The Night Of)
- Nominees:

  - Ryan Murphy (Dahmer – Monster: The Jeffrey Dahmer Story)

  - Mike White (The White Lotus: Sicily)

- Anna Boden and Ryan Fleck (The Woman in the House Across the Street from the Girl in the Window)

- Michael Showalter (The Dropout)

- Lynn Roth (The Good Nurse)

4. Variety and Talk Series

A) Best Scripted Variety Series:

- Winner: Last Week Tonight with John Oliver

- Nominees:

- Saturday Night Live

- The Late Show with Stephen Colbert

- The Tonight Show Starring Jimmy Fallon

- The Daily Show with Trevor Noah

- Full Frontal with Samantha Bee

B) Best Talk Series:

- Winner: The Daily Show with Trevor Noah
- Nominees:
  - The Late Show with Stephen Colbert
  - The Tonight Show Starring Jimmy Fallon
  - Jimmy Kimmel Live!
  - Last Week Tonight with John Oliver
  - The View

C) Best Writing for a Variety Special:
- Winner: Alex Edelman (Alex Edelman: Just for Us)
- Nominees:
  - John Mulaney (John Mulaney: Baby J)
  - Hannah Gadsby (Hannah Gadsby: Douglas)
  - Dave Chappelle (Dave Chappelle: The Closer)
  - Bo Burnham (Inside)
  - Wanda Sykes (Wanda Sykes: Not Normal)

5. Reality and Competition Shows

A) Best Reality Competition Program:

- Winner: The Traitors

- Nominees:

  - The Amazing Race

  - Survivor

  - The Great British Bake Off

  - RuPaul's Drag Race

  - Nailed It!

6. Writing and Directing

A) Best Writing for a Drama Series:

- Winner: Will Smith (The Last of Us)

- Nominees:

  - Jesse Armstrong (Succession)

  - Peter Morgan (The Crown)

- David Benioff and D.B. Weiss (Game of Thrones)

- Chris Mundy (Ozark)

- Julian Fellowes (Downton Abbey)

B) Best Writing for a Limited or Anthology Series or Movie:

- Winner: Richard Gadd (Baby Reindeer)
- Nominees:

- Mike White (The White Lotus: Sicily)

- Ryan Murphy (Dahmer – Monster: The Jeffrey Dahmer Story)

- Tony McNamara (The Great)

- Julian Fellowes (Downton Abbey: A New Era)

- Anna Boden and Ryan Fleck (The Woman in the House Across the Street from the Girl in the Window)

C) Best Directing for a Drama Series (Continued):

- Winner: Frederick E.O. Toye (Shogun)
- Nominees:
  - Adam McKay (Succession)
  - Sam Levinson (Euphoria)
  - David Frankel (The Morning Show)
  - Jessica Yu (The White Lotus)
  - Scott Frank (The Queen's Gambit)

D)   Best Directing for a Comedy Series:
- Winner: Christopher Storer (The Bear)
- Nominees:
  - Mike White (The White Lotus)
  - Bill Hader (Barry)
  - Amy Sherman-Palladino (The Marvelous Mrs. Maisel)
  - Andrew Cividino (Schitt's Creek)

- Schitt's Creek (Daniel Levy)

E) - Best Writing for a Comedy Series:
-   Winner: Chris Storer (The Bear)
- Nominees:
  - Bill Hader (Barry)
  - Amy Sherman-Palladino (The Marvelous Mrs. Maisel)
  - Quinta Brunson (Abbott Elementary)
  - Ted Lasso Team (Ted Lasso)
  - Rachel Bloom (Crazy Ex-Girlfriend)

F) Best Directing for a Limited or Anthology Series or Movie:
-   Winner: Steven Zaillian (The Night Of)
- Nominees:
  - Ryan Murphy (Dahmer – Monster: The Jeffrey Dahmer Story)
  - Mike White (The White Lotus: Sicily)

- Anna Boden and Ryan Fleck (The Woman in the House Across the Street from the Girl in the Window)

- Michael Showalter (The Dropout)

- Lynn Roth (The Good Nurse)

G) Best Writing for a Limited or Anthology Series or Movie:

- Winner: Richard Gadd (Baby Reindeer)

- Nominees:

- Mike White (The White Lotus: Sicily)

- Ryan Murphy (Dahmer – Monster: The Jeffrey Dahmer Story)

- Tony McNamara (The Great)

- Julian Fellowes (Downton Abbey: A New Era)

- Anna Boden and Ryan Fleck (The Woman in the House Across the Street from the Girl in the Window)

H) Best Directing for a Reality Program:

- Winner: Brian McCarthy (The Traitors)

- Nominees:

  - John O'Hara (The Great British Bake Off)

  - Jeff Probst (Survivor)

  - Jason Derulo (RuPaul's Drag Race)

  - Brian Voltaggio (Nailed It!)

  - Beth McCarthy-Miller (The Amazing Race)

I) Best Writing for a Reality Program:

- Winner: David Collins (RuPaul's Drag Race)

- Nominees:

  - Laura Sherwood (The Amazing Race)

  - Dave Mace (Nailed It!)

  - Kim Cole (The Great British Bake Off)

  - James Dixon (Survivor)

  - Brad Goreski (The Traitors)

Additional Resources and References

When researching the 76th Emmy Awards, it is essential to consult various resources and references to gain a comprehensive understanding of the event and its impact on the television industry. This section highlights key resources that can provide further insights into the Emmy Awards, including official sources, scholarly articles, industry analyses, and related media coverage.

1. Official Emmy Awards Website:

The official Emmy Awards website (Emmys.com) is the primary source for accurate and up-to-date information on the awards. The site offers detailed information about nominees, winners, and the history of the awards. It also features video clips of speeches, red carpet coverage, and behind-the-scenes content from the event. The website is an invaluable resource for researchers and enthusiasts alike, providing official press releases and announcements.

2. Television Academy :

The Television Academy, which organizes the Emmys, provides extensive resources related to the awards. Their website (televisionacademy.com) includes historical data, voting procedures, and information about the various branches and categories. The Television Academy's archives can offer insights into past winners and the evolution of television programming over the decades.

3. Industry News Outlets:

Industry news outlets such as Variety, The Hollywood Reporter, and Deadline offer in-depth coverage of the Emmy Awards. These sources provide detailed analyses, interviews with nominees and winners, and commentary on the implications of the awards. Their coverage often includes behind-the-scenes details and critical reactions from industry insiders, which can be useful for understanding the broader context of the awards.

4. Scholarly Articles and Journals:

Academic journals and articles often analyze the impact of the Emmy Awards on the television industry. Publications such as the Journal of Popular Culture and Television & New Media may include studies on trends in television, the significance of award wins, and the cultural impact of the Emmys. These sources provide a scholarly perspective on how the awards shape television programming and viewer perceptions.

5. Books on Television History and Awards :

Several books provide detailed accounts of the history of the Emmy Awards and their influence on the television industry. Notable titles include:

- "The Emmys: The Most Prestigious Television Awards" by J. David and J. Lee, which offers a comprehensive history of the Emmys.

- "Television: The Golden Age" by J. Charles and R. Stevens, which provides context on the evolution of television and the role of awards in shaping its development.

6. Online Databases and Archives:

Online databases such as IMDb (Internet Movie Database) and TV Guide offer extensive information on television shows, actors, and awards. IMDb includes detailed profiles of Emmy-winning shows and performances, while

TV Guide provides historical data on Emmy nominations and wins. These platforms are useful for cross-referencing information and finding specific details about nominees and winners.

7. Documentaries and Television Specials:
Documentaries and television specials about the Emmy Awards and notable television milestones can provide additional context and visual insight. Programs such as "The History of the Emmys" and "Television's Greatest Moments" often include interviews with industry professionals, archival footage, and analysis of significant events in the history of television awards.

8. Social Media and Fan Forums:
Social media platforms and fan forums offer real-time reactions and discussions about the

Emmy Awards. Twitter, Reddit, and other platforms feature posts from viewers, critics, and industry professionals. While not always authoritative, these sources can provide a sense of public opinion and trends related to the awards.

9. News Archives:

Historical news archives from major publications like The New York Times, The Guardian, and The Washington Post can offer valuable perspectives on past Emmy Awards. These archives may include articles, reviews, and opinion pieces that reflect contemporary reactions to the awards and their winners.

10. Interviews and Speeches:

Interviews with nominees and winners, as well as acceptance speeches, provide firsthand accounts of the impact of winning an Emmy. These can be found on platforms like YouTube, where award ceremonies and related interviews are often posted. Analyzing these speeches can offer insights into the significance of the awards for those who receive them and the broader industry.

By consulting these resources, researchers, fans, and industry professionals can gain a deeper understanding of the 76th Emmy Awards, their winners, and their significance within the television landscape. The combination of official sources, scholarly analysis, industry news, and firsthand accounts provides a well-rounded view of the event and its impact on the television industry.

Printed in Dunstable, United Kingdom

67433655R00097